BUILD YOUR OW

A PYTHON DEVELOPER'S TOOLKIT

OLIVER LUCAS JR

TABLE OF CONTENTS

Chapter 1

Chapter 2

Chapter 3

Chapter 4

Chapter 5

Chapter 6

Chapter 7

Chapter 8

Chapter 9

Chapter 10

preface

Welcome to the exciting world of Retrieval Augmented Generation (RAG)! If you're a Python developer eager to explore the cutting edge of AI and build truly intelligent applications, you've come to the right place.

This book is your practical guide to mastering RAG, a powerful technique that combines the strengths of large language models (LLMs) with the vast knowledge stored in external data sources. With RAG, you can create AI systems that are more knowledgeable, accurate, and versatile than ever before.

Why RAG?

Traditional LLMs, while impressive, have limitations. They can hallucinate, generate biased outputs, and lack access to up-to-date information. RAG addresses these challenges by connecting LLMs to a wealth of knowledge, allowing them to retrieve relevant information and generate responses grounded in real-world data.

What You'll Learn

In this book, you'll embark on a hands-on journey to build your own RAG systems from the ground up. You'll learn:

The core concepts of RAG: Retrieval, augmentation, and generation.

Essential Python tools: LangChain, Haystack, FAISS, and other libraries.

Building a knowledge base: Working with text files, PDFs, databases, and APIs.

Mastering retrieval techniques: Dense and sparse retrieval, and hybrid approaches.

Developing RAG applications: Question answering systems, chatbots, and text generation.

Advanced topics: Multi-hop reasoning, handling uncertainty, and explainability.

Who This Book Is For

This book is written for Python developers of all levels who are interested in building AI applications with RAG. Whether you're a beginner or an experienced AI practitioner, you'll find valuable insights and practical guidance to help you get started with RAG.

How to Use This Book

This book is designed to be practical and hands-on. Each chapter builds upon the previous one, guiding you through the process of building your own RAG systems. Code examples are provided throughout the book, allowing you to experiment and apply the concepts you learn.

Join the RAG Revolution

RAG is transforming the way we build AI applications. It's opening up new possibilities for creating intelligent systems that can understand, reason, and generate human-quality text. With this book as your guide, you'll be well-equipped to join the RAG revolution and contribute to the future of AI.

Chapter 1

Introduction to Retrieval Augmented Generation

1.1 The Limitations of LLMs: Why We Need RAG

Large Language Models (LLMs) like GPT-3 and BERT have revolutionized the field of Natural Language Processing (NLP). They can generate human-quality text, translate languages, write different kinds of creative content, and answer your questions in an informative way. However, despite their impressive capabilities, LLMs have some inherent limitations that hinder their ability to truly understand and interact with the world.

1. The Knowledge Cut-Off: LLMs are trained on a massive dataset of text and code, but this dataset has a fixed cut-off point. This means they don't have access to information beyond their training data, making them unaware of recent events, new discoveries, or updates. Imagine asking an LLM about a scientific breakthrough that happened last week – it simply wouldn't know!

2. The Hallucination Problem: LLMs sometimes generate incorrect or nonsensical information, often referred to as "hallucinations." This happens because they learn to predict the next word in a sequence based on patterns in their training data, not based on real-world knowledge or reasoning. While these hallucinations can sometimes be amusing, they can also be misleading and even harmful in certain applications.

3. Lack of Grounding in Real-World Data: LLMs are trained on text, but they don't have a direct connection to the real world. They can't access external databases, interact with APIs, or retrieve information from the web. This limits their ability to answer questions that require factual knowledge or to perform tasks that involve real-world interactions.

4. Difficulty with Complex Reasoning: While LLMs can perform some basic reasoning tasks, they struggle with more complex reasoning that requires multiple steps or the integration of information from different sources. This is because they lack a structured representation of knowledge and rely primarily on statistical patterns in the data.

5. Bias and Ethical Concerns: LLMs can inherit biases present in their training data, leading to unfair or discriminatory outputs. This is a serious concern, especially in applications where LLMs are used to make decisions that affect people's lives.

Enter Retrieval Augmented Generation (RAG)

These limitations of LLMs highlight the need for a new approach that combines the power of language generation with the ability to access and reason over external knowledge sources. This is where Retrieval Augmented Generation (RAG) comes in.

RAG addresses the limitations of LLMs by:

Connecting LLMs to a knowledge base: RAG systems can access and retrieve relevant information from a variety of sources, including documents, databases, and APIs, providing LLMs with up-to-date and grounded knowledge.

Reducing hallucinations: By grounding the LLM's responses in retrieved information, RAG can significantly reduce the likelihood of generating incorrect or nonsensical outputs.

Enabling more complex reasoning: RAG allows LLMs to perform multi-step reasoning by retrieving and integrating information from multiple sources.

Improving explainability: RAG systems can provide insights into how they arrived at a particular answer by showing the retrieved information that supports their response.

1.2 The Core Concepts of RAG: Retrieval, Augmentation, Generation

Retrieval Augmented Generation, at its heart, is a clever combination of three key processes:

1. Retrieval:

Finding the Right Information: Imagine your knowledge base as a vast library. Retrieval is like having a super-efficient librarian who can instantly find the most relevant books (or documents) related to your query.

Going Beyond Keywords: Instead of just matching keywords, RAG uses intelligent retrieval methods to understand the *meaning* of your query and find documents with similar semantic meaning. This often involves techniques like:

Embeddings: Representing text as numerical vectors that capture their meaning.

Vector Databases: Storing and efficiently searching these embeddings.

Similarity Search: Finding documents whose embeddings are closest to the query's embedding.

Python Tools: Libraries like FAISS, Milvus, and Redis are commonly used for efficient similarity search in RAG systems.

2. Augmentation:

Enriching the Context: Once the relevant information is retrieved, it's used to *augment* the prompt given to the language model. This is like giving the LLM extra context or background knowledge to help it generate a better response.

Different Augmentation Strategies:

Include relevant text snippets directly in the prompt: This provides the LLM with specific information to draw upon.

Summarize the retrieved documents: This gives the LLM a condensed overview of the key points.

Create a knowledge graph from the retrieved data: This provides a structured representation of the information.

The Goal: Augmentation ensures the LLM has the necessary information to generate a response that is accurate, relevant, and grounded in the knowledge base.

3. Generation:

The LLM's Role: This is where the language model shines. It takes the augmented prompt and generates the final output, whether it's an answer to a question, a summary of a document, or a creative piece of writing.

Leveraging LLM Strengths: RAG leverages the LLM's ability to:

Understand natural language: Interpreting the query and the retrieved information.

Generate human-quality text: Producing fluent and coherent responses.

Adapt to different tasks: Performing various tasks like question answering, summarization, and dialogue generation.

Python Tools: Popular LLMs like GPT-3 (accessed via OpenAI's API), or open-source models like Flan-T5 and OPT, can be used for the generation step.

The Power of the Combination:

By combining these three processes, RAG systems create a powerful synergy between information retrieval and language generation. This leads to AI systems that are:

More Knowledgeable: They can access and utilize a vast amount of information.

More Accurate: They are less prone to hallucinations and provide grounded responses.

More Versatile: They can be adapted to a wide range of applications.

1.3 Real-World Applications: From Chatbots to Question Answering

RAG is quickly becoming a go-to technology for building AI systems that are more knowledgeable, accurate, and versatile. Let's explore some of its most exciting applications:

1. Intelligent Chatbots:

Beyond Scripted Responses: Traditional chatbots often rely on pre-defined rules and struggle with complex or unexpected questions. RAG empowers chatbots to:

Access and retrieve information from company knowledge bases, product documentation, or even the entire web.

Provide dynamic and contextually relevant answers.

Engage in more natural and informative conversations.

Example: A customer support chatbot for an e-commerce company can use RAG to answer questions about specific products, order statuses, or return policies by retrieving information from the company's databases and FAQs.

2. Advanced Question Answering Systems:

Accurate and Comprehensive Answers: RAG enables question answering systems to go beyond simple keyword matching and provide more accurate and comprehensive answers.

Handling Complex Questions: RAG systems can handle complex questions that require:

Multi-step reasoning (e.g., "What is the capital of the country where the Eiffel Tower is located?")

Information from multiple sources (e.g., "Compare the features of the latest iPhone and Samsung Galaxy phone.")

Example: A research assistant tool can use RAG to answer questions by retrieving information from scientific papers, research databases, and online encyclopedias.

3. Personalized Content Recommendation:

Understanding User Preferences: RAG can be used to build recommendation systems that understand user preferences and provide personalized content suggestions.

Going Beyond Collaborative Filtering: By analyzing the content of articles, books, or movies, RAG can identify items that are semantically similar to what a user has liked in the past.

Example: A news aggregator app can use RAG to recommend articles that are relevant to a user's interests based on their reading history and the content of the articles.

4. Knowledge Management and Discovery:

Unlocking Insights from Data: Many organizations have vast amounts of data stored in documents, reports, and databases. RAG can help unlock valuable insights from this data by:

Making it easily searchable.

Summarizing key information.

Identifying connections and patterns.

Example: A legal team can use RAG to quickly find relevant case law, legal precedents, and expert opinions within a vast collection of legal documents.

5. Code Generation and Autocompletion:

AI-Powered Coding Assistants: RAG can be used to build coding assistants that:

Suggest relevant code snippets based on the current context.

Generate code for common tasks.

Help developers find information in documentation and online forums.

Example: A code editor plugin can use RAG to suggest code completions, provide explanations of functions, and retrieve examples of how to use specific libraries.

Beyond these examples: RAG is also being applied in fields like education, healthcare, finance, and more. Its ability to combine the power of language models with external knowledge sources opens up a world of possibilities for building AI systems that are truly helpful and informative.

Chapter 2

Setting Up Your RAG Development Environment

2.1 Essential Python Libraries: LangChain, Haystack, FAISS

Python's rich ecosystem of libraries makes it a perfect language for building RAG applications. Here are three essential libraries that will be your companions throughout this journey:

1. LangChain:

The Orchestrator: LangChain is a powerful framework designed specifically for developing applications powered by large language models. It provides a simple and standardized way to:

Chain together different components: Connect LLMs with other tools and data sources.

Manage prompts: Create and manage prompts effectively, including dynamic prompts that incorporate retrieved context.

Access various LLMs: Integrate with different language models, whether they are open-source or accessed via APIs (like OpenAI's GPT models).

Work with different data sources: Connect to various data sources, including vector databases, APIs, and document loaders.

Why it's Essential for RAG: LangChain simplifies many of the common tasks involved in building RAG systems, such as managing prompts, interacting with LLMs, and chaining together retrieval and generation steps.

2. Haystack:

End-to-End Framework: Haystack is an open-source framework specifically designed for building search systems, including question answering systems that leverage RAG. It provides:

Modular components: Flexible components for different parts of the RAG pipeline, such as document storage, retrieval, and readers (which extract answers from retrieved documents).

Pre-trained models: Access to pre-trained models for retrieval and question answering.

Pipeline customization: Ability to customize the pipeline to fit your specific needs.

Evaluation tools: Tools for evaluating the performance of your RAG system.

Why it's Essential for RAG: Haystack provides a comprehensive set of tools for building and deploying production-ready RAG systems, especially for question answering applications.

3. FAISS:

Efficient Similarity Search: FAISS (Facebook AI Similarity Search) is a library that specializes in efficient similarity search and clustering of dense vectors.

Handling Large Datasets: FAISS is designed to handle massive datasets of vectors, making it ideal for storing and searching document embeddings in RAG systems.

Optimized for Performance: FAISS provides highly optimized algorithms for similarity search, ensuring fast retrieval even with millions of documents.

GPU Support: FAISS can leverage GPUs to further accelerate search, which is crucial for large-scale RAG applications.

Why it's Essential for RAG: Efficient retrieval is crucial for RAG performance, and FAISS provides the tools to achieve that efficiency, especially when dealing with large knowledge bases.

Getting Started:

To start building your RAG applications, you'll need to install these libraries:

Bash

```
pip install langchain haystack faiss
```

(Note: For GPU support in FAISS, you may need to install `faiss-gpu` instead of `faiss`)

In the next section, we'll explore how to use these libraries to access external knowledge sources through APIs, further expanding the capabilities of your RAG systems.

2.2 Working with APIs: Accessing External Knowledge Sources

APIs (Application Programming Interfaces) are the gateways to a treasure trove of external knowledge. They allow your RAG systems to tap into real-time information, specialized databases, and powerful services. Here's how you can leverage APIs in your Python-based RAG applications:

1. Finding the Right APIs:

Identify Your Needs: What kind of external knowledge do you need?

General Knowledge: Wikipedia API, Google Knowledge Graph API

News and Current Events: New York Times API, Twitter API

Scientific Data: PubMed API, arXiv API

Financial Data: Yahoo Finance API, Alpha Vantage API

Explore API Marketplaces: Websites like RapidAPI and ProgrammableWeb provide directories of thousands of APIs.

2. Making API Requests with Python:

The `requests` Library: Python's `requests` library is your go-to tool for making HTTP requests to APIs.

Python

```python
import requests

response = requests.get('https://api.example.com/data')
data = response.json()
print(data)
```

Handling API Keys and Authentication: Many APIs require authentication. You'll often need to include an API key in your requests.

Python

```
headers = {
    'Authorization': 'Bearer YOUR_API_KEY'
}
response                                    =
requests.get('https://api.example.com/data',
headers=headers)
```

Parsing API Responses: API responses often come in JSON format. You can use Python's `json` library to parse the data.

3. Integrating APIs with LangChain:

LangChain's API Wrappers: LangChain provides convenient wrappers for many popular APIs, making it easy to integrate them into your RAG pipeline.

Python

```
from          langchain.utilities          import
WikipediaAPIWrapper

wikipedia = WikipediaAPIWrapper()
result = wikipedia.run('Albert Einstein')
print(result)
```

Custom API Chains: You can create custom chains in LangChain to combine API calls with LLMs. For example, you could create a chain that first retrieves information from a news API and then uses an LLM to summarize the news.

4. Example: Building a RAG System with a News API

Let's say you want to build a system that answers questions about recent news events. Here's a basic example using LangChain and a hypothetical news API:

Python

```python
from langchain import PromptTemplate, LLMChain
from langchain.llms import OpenAI
from langchain.utilities import NewsAPIWrapper

# Initialize the News API wrapper (replace with
your actual API key)
news_api                                            =
NewsAPIWrapper(api_key="YOUR_NEWS_API_KEY")

# Create a prompt template
template = """
Use the following news information to answer the
user's question:

{news_results}

Question: {question}
Answer:"""
prompt      =      PromptTemplate(template=template,
input_variables=["news_results", "question"])

# Initialize the LLM
llm = OpenAI(temperature=0)
```

```
# Create the LLM chain
llm_chain = LLMChain(prompt=prompt, llm=llm)

# Get news results from the API
question = "What are the latest developments in
artificial intelligence?"
news_results = news_api.run(question)

# Run the LLM chain with the retrieved news data
response       =       llm_chain.run({'news_results':
news_results, 'question': question})
print(response)
```

Important Considerations:

API Limits and Rate Limiting: Be mindful of API usage limits and implement strategies to handle rate limiting.

Error Handling: Include robust error handling to gracefully manage API errors.

Data Security: Protect sensitive API keys and data.

By incorporating APIs into your RAG systems, you can create truly dynamic and informative applications that have access to a wealth of real-world knowledge.

2.3 Choosing Your IDE and Tools: Streamlining Your Workflow

The right Integrated Development Environment (IDE) and a set of helpful tools can significantly boost your productivity and make RAG development smoother and more enjoyable. Here's a guide to help you choose the best options for your needs:

1. Selecting Your IDE:

Popular Choices for Python:

VS Code: A lightweight yet powerful open-source editor with excellent Python support, a vast extension marketplace, and great community support.

PyCharm: A feature-rich IDE specifically designed for Python development, offering advanced debugging, code analysis, and refactoring tools.

Jupyter Notebook/Lab: Ideal for interactive development and experimentation, especially when working with data exploration, visualization, and machine learning tasks related to RAG.

Key Features to Consider:

Intelligent Code Completion: Helps you write code faster and with fewer errors.

Debugging Capabilities: Essential for identifying and fixing issues in your RAG pipeline.

Integrated Terminal: Allows you to run commands and scripts without leaving the IDE.

Version Control Integration: Seamlessly integrates with Git for managing your codebase.

Extensions and Plugins: Expand the functionality of your IDE with tools for specific tasks, like LangChain or Haystack integration.

2. Essential Tools for RAG Development:

Environment Management:

conda or venv: Create isolated environments to manage dependencies for different RAG projects.

Code Formatting:

Black: Automatically formats your Python code to adhere to style guidelines, improving readability and consistency.

Testing:

pytest: A popular testing framework for writing and running tests to ensure the quality and reliability of your RAG system.

Experiment Tracking:

MLflow or Weights & Biases: Track experiments, log metrics, and visualize results to optimize your RAG pipeline.

3. Streamlining Your Workflow:

Keyboard Shortcuts: Learn and utilize keyboard shortcuts to navigate, edit, and execute code quickly.

Code Snippets: Create reusable code snippets for common tasks, such as making API requests or processing data.

Debugging Techniques: Master debugging techniques like setting breakpoints, stepping through code, and inspecting variables.

Collaboration Tools: Utilize Git for version control and collaborate effectively with other developers on RAG projects.

Example: Setting Up VS Code for RAG Development

1 Install the Python Extension: Provides essential features like code completion, linting, and debugging.

2 Install the LangChain Extension: Offers helpful features like code completion and navigation for LangChain.

3 Configure a Virtual Environment: Use the integrated terminal to create and activate a virtual environment using `conda` or `venv`.

4 Install Required Libraries: Use `pip` to install LangChain, Haystack, FAISS, and other necessary libraries within the virtual environment.

5 Customize Settings: Adjust settings for code formatting, linting, and other preferences.

By carefully selecting your IDE and tools, and by adopting efficient workflows, you can create a development environment that maximizes your productivity and helps you build robust and innovative RAG applications.

Chapter 3

Building Your Knowledge Base

3.1 Data Sources: Text Files, PDFs, Databases, APIs

The foundation of any powerful RAG system is a well-structured and comprehensive knowledge base. Fortunately, you can draw from a wide variety of data sources to build this foundation. Here's a breakdown of common data source types and how to work with them in Python:

1. Text Files:

Simple and Versatile: Plain text files (.txt) are a straightforward way to store information. They're easy to create, edit, and process.

Python Tools:

Open and Read: Use Python's built-in `open()` function to read the contents of text files.

Python

```
with open('my_document.txt', 'r') as file:

    text = file.read()
```

Process Line by Line: Iterate through the lines of a text file for line-by-line processing.

Python

```python
with open('my_document.txt', 'r') as file:

    for line in file:

        # Process each line
```

2. PDFs:

Widely Used: PDFs (.pdf) are a standard format for documents, often containing rich formatting and images.

Python Tools:

PyPDF2: Extract text content from PDFs.

Python

```python
import PyPDF2


with open('my_document.pdf', 'rb') as pdf_file:

    reader = PyPDF2.PdfReader(pdf_file)

    text = ""

    for page in reader.pages:

        text += page.extract_text()
```

Other Libraries: Explore libraries like pdfplumber or camelot for more advanced PDF processing, such as extracting tables and structured data.

3. Databases:

Structured Data: Databases (SQL or NoSQL) are excellent for storing structured data with relationships between different pieces of information.

Python Tools:

Database Connectors: Use libraries like `sqlite3` (for SQLite), `psycopg2` (for PostgreSQL), or `pymongo` (for MongoDB) to connect to and query databases.

Python

```python
import sqlite3


conn = sqlite3.connect('my_database.db')

cursor = conn.cursor()

cursor.execute("SELECT * FROM my_table")

results = cursor.fetchall()
```

SQLAlchemy: An Object-Relational Mapper (ORM) that provides a higher-level interface for interacting with databases.

4. APIs:

Real-time and Dynamic Data: APIs provide access to a vast range of external data sources, including news feeds, social media, scientific data, and more.

Python Tools:

requests: The standard Python library for making HTTP requests to APIs.

LangChain API Wrappers: Simplify interaction with common APIs like Wikipedia or Google Search.

5. Choosing the Right Data Source:

Data Structure: Is your data structured (like in a database) or unstructured (like in a text file)?

Data Volume: How much data do you need to store and process?

Data Updates: How often does the data need to be updated?

Access Methods: How will you access and retrieve the data?

3.2 Data Preprocessing: Cleaning, Formatting, and Structuring

Raw data is often messy, inconsistent, and full of noise. Before you can feed it to your RAG system, you need to whip it into shape! Data preprocessing involves a series of steps to clean, format, and structure your data, ensuring it's optimized for retrieval and generation.

1. Cleaning:

Handling Missing Values:

Identify Missing Data: Use libraries like Pandas to identify missing values (often represented as NaN or null).

Strategies:

Removal: Remove rows or columns with missing data (if feasible).

Imputation: Fill in missing values with estimated values (e.g., mean, median, or using more sophisticated imputation techniques).

Removing Duplicates:

Identify Duplicates: Use Pandas functions like `duplicated()` and `drop_duplicates()` to find and remove duplicate entries.

Correcting Errors:

Typos and Inconsistent Formatting: Use regular expressions and string manipulation techniques to correct typos, standardize capitalization, and ensure consistent formatting.

2. Formatting:

Text Normalization:

Lowercasing: Convert all text to lowercase to ensure case-insensitive matching.

Removing Punctuation: Remove or standardize punctuation depending on your needs.

Stemming and Lemmatization: Reduce words to their root form (e.g., "running" to "run") using libraries like NLTK.

Data Type Conversion:

Ensure Correct Types: Make sure numerical data is represented as numbers, dates are in datetime format, etc.

3. Structuring:

Chunking:

Divide Long Documents: Break down large documents into smaller chunks to improve retrieval efficiency and context window management for LLMs.

Strategies: Divide by paragraphs, sections, or a fixed number of words.

Creating Metadata:

Add Contextual Information: Add metadata to your data, such as document titles, authors, dates, or keywords. This metadata can be used for filtering and retrieval.

Python Tools for Data Preprocessing:

Pandas: A powerful library for data manipulation and analysis, offering functions for cleaning, transforming, and structuring data.

NLTK: The Natural Language Toolkit provides tools for text processing tasks like tokenization, stemming, and lemmatization.

Regular Expressions: Use Python's re module for pattern matching and text cleaning.

Example: Cleaning and Formatting Text Data

Python

```python
import pandas as pd

import re

from nltk.stem import WordNetLemmatizer


# Sample text data

text = "This is an Example with Some!  errors and
duplicate words words."


# Lowercase
```

```python
text = text.lower()


# Remove punctuation

text = re.sub(r'[^\w\s]', '', text)


# Remove duplicate words

words = text.split()

text         =         '         '.join(sorted(set(words),
key=words.index))


# Lemmatization

lemmatizer = WordNetLemmatizer()

text = ' '.join([lemmatizer.lemmatize(word)  for
word in text.split()])



print(text)   # Output:  this  is  an  example  with
some error and duplicate word
```

By diligently preprocessing your data, you can create a clean, organized, and efficient knowledge base that will significantly enhance the performance and accuracy of your RAG system.

3.3 Indexing for Efficient Retrieval: Vector Databases and Search

Imagine searching through a library with millions of books. Looking at each book one by one would take forever! That's where indexing comes in. In the context of RAG, indexing helps you quickly find the most relevant information within your knowledge base.

1. Why Vector Databases?

Beyond Keyword Search: Traditional databases rely on keyword matching, which can be limited when dealing with complex language and semantic meaning.

Capturing Meaning: Vector databases store data as embeddings (numerical vectors that represent the meaning of text). This allows for semantic search, finding documents with similar meanings even if they don't share the exact same keywords.

Efficient Similarity Search: Vector databases are optimized for finding the "nearest neighbors" to a given query embedding, making them ideal for RAG retrieval.

2. Popular Vector Databases:

FAISS: A library developed by Facebook AI Research, highly optimized for similarity search and clustering of dense vectors.

Milvus: An open-source vector database designed for large-scale similarity search, with support for various indexing methods.

Pinecone: A managed vector database service that offers scalability, reliability, and ease of use.

Redis: While primarily known as a key-value store, Redis also offers modules for vector similarity search.

Chroma: An open-source embedding database specifically designed for LLM applications, with a focus on ease of use and developer experience.

3. Indexing Techniques:

Vector databases employ various indexing techniques to speed up similarity search. Here are a few common ones:

Flat Index (Brute-force): Calculates the distance between the query vector and every vector in the database. Simple but slow for large datasets.

Inverted File Index (IVF): Divides the data into clusters and only searches within the most relevant clusters.

Hierarchical Navigable Small World (HNSW): Creates a graph-like structure that allows for efficient approximate nearest neighbor search.

Product Quantization (PQ): Compresses the vectors to reduce storage space and speed up calculations.

4. Choosing the Right Vector Database and Index:

Dataset Size: How large is your knowledge base?

Performance Requirements: What are your latency requirements for retrieval?

Scalability Needs: Will your knowledge base grow significantly over time?

Budget: Are you looking for an open-source solution or a managed service?

Ease of Use: How easy is it to set up, manage, and integrate the database?

5. Example: Using FAISS for Similarity Search

Python

```python
import faiss

import numpy as np


# Sample embeddings (replace with your actual
embeddings)

embeddings          =          np.random.rand(1000,
128).astype('float32')


# Create a FlatL2 index (for small datasets)

index = faiss.IndexFlatL2(128)    # 128 is the
dimensionality of the embeddings


# Add the embeddings to the index

index.add(embeddings)


# Search for the nearest neighbors to a query
embedding

query_embedding          =          np.random.rand(1,
128).astype('float32')

D, I = index.search(query_embedding, k=5)    # k is
the number of neighbors to retrieve
```

```
# D contains the distances, I contains the
indices of the nearest neighbors

print(I)
```

By understanding vector databases, indexing techniques, and the tools available in Python, you can build a RAG system that efficiently retrieves the most relevant information from your knowledge base, even when dealing with massive amounts of data.

Chapter 4

Mastering Retrieval Techniques

4.1 Dense Retrieval: Embeddings and Semantic Similarity

Dense retrieval is a powerful technique that moves beyond simple keyword matching to truly understand the *meaning* behind your queries and documents. It does this through the magic of embeddings and semantic similarity.

1. Embeddings: Capturing Meaning in Vectors

Representing Text as Numbers: Embeddings are dense vectors (lists of numbers) that represent words, sentences, or even entire documents in a multi-dimensional space.

Capturing Semantic Relationships: The key is that these vectors are positioned in the space such that words or documents with similar meanings are closer together. For example, the embeddings for "king" and "queen" would be closer than the embeddings for "king" and "table."

Generating Embeddings: You can generate embeddings using powerful language models like:

Sentence-BERT: Specifically designed for generating sentence and document embeddings.

all-mpnet-base-v2: A general-purpose language model that produces high-quality embeddings.

OpenAI Embeddings API: Provides access to OpenAI's powerful embedding models.

2. Semantic Similarity

Measuring Meaning: Once you have embeddings for your query and documents, you can calculate the semantic similarity between them.

Cosine Similarity: A common measure of similarity is the cosine similarity, which calculates the cosine of the angle between two vectors. A cosine similarity of 1 means the vectors are identical, while 0 means they are completely dissimilar.

Finding the Nearest Neighbors: Dense retrieval involves finding the documents in your knowledge base whose embeddings have the highest cosine similarity to the query embedding. These documents are considered the most semantically similar to the query.

3. The Dense Retrieval Process

1 Embed the Query: Generate an embedding for the user's query.

2 Embed the Documents: (This is often done beforehand and stored in a vector database).

3 Calculate Similarity: Calculate the cosine similarity between the query embedding and all document embeddings.

4 Retrieve the Nearest Neighbors: Return the documents with the highest similarity scores.

4. Advantages of Dense Retrieval:

Captures Semantic Meaning: Goes beyond keyword matching to understand the intent and context of the query.

Handles Variations in Language: Can find relevant documents even if they use different wording or synonyms.

Effective for Complex Queries: Performs well with complex or ambiguous queries.

5. Example: Calculating Cosine Similarity in Python

Python

```python
import numpy as np

from        sklearn.metrics.pairwise        import
cosine_similarity


# Sample embeddings

embedding1 = np.array([0.1, 0.2, 0.3])

embedding2 = np.array([0.4, 0.5, 0.6])


# Calculate cosine similarity

similarity    =    cosine_similarity([embedding1],
[embedding2])


print(similarity)  # Output: [[0.97463185]]
```

By understanding embeddings and semantic similarity, and by leveraging powerful vector databases and libraries like FAISS, you can implement dense retrieval in your RAG systems to achieve more accurate and relevant information retrieval.

4.2 Sparse Retrieval: TF-IDF and Keyword Matching

Sparse retrieval techniques, like TF-IDF, focus on identifying relevant documents based on the presence and importance of specific keywords in both the query and the documents. These methods are often simpler to implement and understand compared to dense retrieval, and they can be very effective, especially for large datasets.

1. TF-IDF: Weighing the Importance of Words

TF-IDF stands for Term Frequency-Inverse Document Frequency. It's a numerical statistic that reflects how important a word is to a document in a collection of documents.

Term Frequency (TF): Measures how frequently a term appears in a document. A higher TF indicates that the term is more important within that document.

Inverse Document Frequency (IDF): Measures how rare a term is across the entire collection of documents. A higher IDF indicates that the term is more unique and discriminative.

The TF-IDF Score: Calculated by multiplying TF and IDF. A high TF-IDF score means that a word appears often in a document but is relatively rare across the entire corpus, suggesting it's a good keyword for that document.

2. Keyword Matching

Identifying Shared Keywords: Sparse retrieval often involves identifying keywords that are present in both the query and the documents.

Boolean Retrieval: A simple approach uses Boolean operators (AND, OR, NOT) to combine keywords and find documents that match specific criteria. For example, a query for "Python AND machine learning" would retrieve documents containing both keywords.

3. The Sparse Retrieval Process

1 Tokenize: Break down the query and documents into individual words (tokens).

2 Calculate TF-IDF: Calculate the TF-IDF score for each term in each document.

3 Match Keywords: Identify keywords shared between the query and the documents.

4 Rank Documents: Rank documents based on the TF-IDF scores of the matched keywords or other relevance metrics (like BM25, a more advanced ranking function).

4. Advantages of Sparse Retrieval

Efficiency: Can be very efficient for large datasets, as it often involves simpler calculations than dense retrieval.

Interpretability: The results are easy to understand, as you can see which keywords led to a document being retrieved.

No Training Data Required: TF-IDF doesn't require training data, unlike embedding models used in dense retrieval.

5. Example: Calculating TF-IDF in Python

Python

```
from    sklearn.feature_extraction.text    import
TfidfVectorizer


# Sample documents

documents = [

    "This is the first document.",

    "This document is the second document.",

    "And this is the third one.",

]
```

```
# Create a TF-IDF vectorizer

vectorizer = TfidfVectorizer()


# Fit the vectorizer to the documents

tfidf_matrix                                              =
vectorizer.fit_transform(documents)


# Print the TF-IDF matrix

print(tfidf_matrix.toarray())
```

By understanding TF-IDF, keyword matching, and the tools available in libraries like scikit-learn, you can implement sparse retrieval methods in your RAG systems to efficiently find relevant information, especially when dealing with large collections of text data.

4.3 Hybrid Approaches: Combining Dense and Sparse Methods

While dense and sparse retrieval each have their strengths, combining them in a hybrid approach can often lead to even more effective and robust RAG systems. This allows you to leverage the semantic understanding of dense retrieval and the efficiency and interpretability of sparse retrieval.

1. Why Combine Dense and Sparse?

Improved Recall: Sparse retrieval (e.g., keyword matching) can ensure that you don't miss documents containing important keywords, while dense retrieval can find semantically similar documents even if they don't have exact keyword matches.

Increased Precision: Dense retrieval can help filter out documents that match keywords but are not semantically relevant, improving the precision of the results.

Balanced Performance: Combining methods can help balance the trade-off between accuracy, efficiency, and interpretability.

2. Common Hybrid Approaches

Rank Fusion:

Retrieve with Both Methods: Retrieve a set of candidate documents using both dense and sparse retrieval.

Combine Scores: Combine the scores from both methods (e.g., by averaging or weighted averaging) to create a final ranking.

Two-Stage Retrieval:

Stage 1 (Sparse): Use sparse retrieval (e.g., TF-IDF) to quickly narrow down the search space to a smaller set of candidates.

Stage 2 (Dense): Apply dense retrieval to the candidate set to re-rank them based on semantic similarity.

Combining Embeddings and Keyword Information:

Augment Embeddings: Incorporate keyword information into the embedding space to create "hybrid" embeddings that capture both semantic meaning and keyword relevance.

3. Example: Hybrid Retrieval with LangChain

LangChain provides tools for combining retrieval methods. Here's a basic example of how you might combine a keyword-based retriever with an embedding-based retriever:

Python

```python
from langchain.retrievers import TFIDFRetriever, FAISSRetriever

from langchain.chains import RetrievalQA


# Load your data and create the retrievers

# ... (Code to load data and create TFIDFRetriever and FAISSRetriever) ...


# Combine the retrievers

hybrid_retriever = TFIDFRetriever.from_texts(texts) + FAISSRetriever.from_texts(texts)


# Create a RetrievalQA chain with the hybrid retriever

qa_chain = RetrievalQA.from_chain_type(llm=llm, retriever=hybrid_retriever)


# Run the chain
```

```
query = "What is the capital of France?"

result = qa_chain({"query": query})

print(result)
```

4. Choosing the Right Hybrid Approach

The best hybrid approach will depend on your specific needs and the characteristics of your data. Consider factors like:

Dataset Size: For very large datasets, a two-stage approach might be more efficient.

Query Complexity: For complex queries, dense retrieval might play a more important role.

Interpretability Needs: If interpretability is crucial, you might give more weight to sparse retrieval scores.

By carefully combining dense and sparse methods, you can create RAG systems that are both accurate and efficient, providing the best possible retrieval performance for your applications.

Chapter 5

Working with Language Models

5.1 Choosing the Right LLM: Open Source vs. Commercial APIs

The "generation" step in RAG relies heavily on the capabilities of your chosen Large Language Model (LLM). You have two primary options: open-source models that you can run yourself, or commercial APIs that provide access to powerful LLMs hosted by companies like OpenAI or Google.

1. Open-Source LLMs

Flexibility and Customization:

Full Control: You have complete control over the model, allowing for fine-tuning, modification, and customization to your specific needs.

Data Privacy: You can run the model on your own infrastructure, ensuring data privacy and security, which is crucial for sensitive applications.

Cost-Effectiveness:

No Usage Fees: You avoid the usage fees associated with commercial APIs, making it potentially more cost-effective, especially for high-volume applications.

Community and Collaboration:

Active Development: Open-source models often have active communities of developers contributing to their improvement and sharing knowledge.

Examples:

Flan-T5: A family of encoder-decoder models from Google, known for good performance across a variety of tasks.

OPT: A series of decoder-only models from Meta, offering various sizes and capabilities.

BLOOM: A large multilingual language model developed by a collaborative research effort.

2. Commercial LLM APIs

Ease of Use:

Simple Integration: APIs provide a straightforward way to integrate LLMs into your applications without the need for complex setup or infrastructure management.

State-of-the-Art Performance:

Access to Cutting-Edge Models: Companies like OpenAI and Google invest heavily in developing and training large, powerful LLMs that are often at the forefront of language technology.

Support and Reliability:

Documentation and Community: Commercial APIs typically come with comprehensive documentation, support resources, and active developer communities.

Reliable Infrastructure: You benefit from the robust and scalable infrastructure of the API provider.

Examples:

OpenAI API: Provides access to models like GPT-3, GPT-4, and Codex.

Google AI Platform: Offers various language models for different tasks, including text generation, translation, and dialogue.

Cohere API: Provides access to powerful LLMs for text generation, classification, and more.

3. Making the Choice

Performance Needs: If you need the absolute best performance, commercial APIs often have the edge with their large and highly trained models.

Customization Requirements: If you need to heavily customize or fine-tune the model, open-source is the way to go.

Cost Considerations: Factor in the cost of API usage fees versus the cost of running and maintaining an open-source model.

Data Privacy: If data privacy is paramount, running an open-source model on your own infrastructure is essential.

Ease of Integration: If you prioritize ease of integration, commercial APIs offer a simpler solution.

4. Hybrid Approach

Best of Both Worlds: You can even combine open-source and commercial APIs in a hybrid approach. For example, you might use an open-source model for certain tasks or during development and then switch to a commercial API for production when you need higher performance or specific capabilities.

By carefully considering these factors, you can choose the LLM solution that best fits the needs of your RAG application.

5.2 Prompt Engineering for RAG: Guiding the LLM's Output

In RAG, prompt engineering takes on even greater importance. You're not just guiding the LLM to generate text; you're guiding it to generate text that is grounded in the information retrieved from your knowledge base. Here's how to craft effective prompts for RAG:

1. Provide Context with Retrieved Information

Include Relevant Snippets: Incorporate the most relevant snippets of text retrieved from your knowledge base directly into the prompt. This gives the LLM specific information to draw upon.

Summarize Key Findings: If you've retrieved multiple documents, provide a concise summary of the key points in the prompt.

Structure the Information: Use formatting (like bullet points, headings, or tables) to structure the retrieved information and make it easier for the LLM to process.

2. Give Clear Instructions

Specify the Task: Clearly state the task you want the LLM to perform (e.g., "Answer the following question based on the provided context," or "Summarize the following information").

Define the Desired Output: Be specific about the format and type of output you expect (e.g., "Provide a short answer in one sentence," or "Generate a list of bullet points").

Set Constraints: If necessary, set constraints on the output length, style, or tone.

3. Refine and Iterate

Experiment with Different Prompts: Try different prompt structures and wording to see what works best for your specific task and LLM.

Analyze the Output: Carefully examine the LLM's output to identify areas where the prompt can be improved.

Iterative Refinement: Refine your prompts based on the LLM's responses to achieve the desired output quality and relevance.

4. Example: Prompt for a Question Answering System

```
## Context:
```

```
*   **Document  1:**   "Paris  is  the  capital  of
France..."
```

```
*   **Document  2:**    "France  is  a  country  in
Europe..."
```

```
## Question: What is the capital of France?
```

```
## Answer:
```

In this example, the prompt provides the LLM with context from retrieved documents and clearly states the question to be answered.

5. Advanced Prompt Engineering Techniques

Few-Shot Learning: Provide a few examples of the desired input-output pairs in the prompt to guide the LLM.

Chain-of-Thought Prompting: Encourage the LLM to generate a step-by-step reasoning process before providing the final answer.

Prompt Engineering Frameworks: Explore tools like LangChain, which provide features for managing and optimizing prompts.

By mastering prompt engineering techniques, you can effectively guide the LLM in your RAG system to generate accurate, relevant, and informative outputs that are grounded in your knowledge base.

5.3 Fine-tuning LLMs for Specific Tasks

While pre-trained LLMs possess impressive general language abilities, fine-tuning allows you to adapt them to excel in specific tasks and domains relevant to your RAG application. This process refines the LLM's parameters by training it on a smaller, focused dataset, leading to significant improvements in accuracy, relevance, and efficiency.

1. Why Fine-tune?

Enhanced Performance: Fine-tuning improves the LLM's ability to perform the target task, leading to more accurate and relevant outputs.

Domain Adaptation: You can adapt the LLM to a specific domain or knowledge area, making it more knowledgeable and effective within that context.

Reduced Hallucinations: Fine-tuning can help reduce the likelihood of the LLM generating incorrect or nonsensical information.

Improved Efficiency: A fine-tuned LLM may require fewer tokens or less processing time to achieve the desired output.

2. The Fine-tuning Process

1 Gather a Task-Specific Dataset: Create a dataset of input-output pairs that are representative of the specific task you want the LLM to perform.

2 Choose a Base LLM: Select a pre-trained LLM as your starting point. Consider factors like model size, performance, and availability.

3 Fine-tune the LLM: Train the LLM on your task-specific dataset, adjusting the model's parameters to optimize its performance on the target task.

4 Evaluate and Iterate: Evaluate the fine-tuned LLM's performance and iterate on the process by adjusting the training data, hyperparameters, or base LLM to achieve the desired results.

3. Fine-tuning Techniques

Instruction Tuning: Fine-tune the LLM on a dataset of instructions and corresponding desired outputs. This helps the model better understand and follow instructions within your RAG system.

Supervised Fine-tuning (SFT): Train the LLM on a labeled dataset to predict specific outputs for given inputs. This is useful for tasks like question answering or text summarization.

Parameter-Efficient Fine-tuning (PEFT): Fine-tune only a small subset of the LLM's parameters, making the process more efficient and reducing storage requirements.

4. Tools and Resources

Hugging Face Transformers: A popular library that provides tools for fine-tuning a wide variety of LLMs.

OpenAI Fine-tuning API: Allows you to fine-tune GPT-3 models for specific tasks.

Google AI Platform: Provides resources and infrastructure for fine-tuning LLMs on Google Cloud.

5. Example: Fine-tuning for Question Answering

Imagine you're building a RAG system to answer questions about a specific domain, like medical information. You could fine-tune an LLM on a dataset of medical questions and answers to improve its accuracy and relevance in that domain.

Important Considerations

Dataset Quality: The quality of your fine-tuning dataset is crucial. Ensure it's accurate, representative, and sufficiently large.

Computational Resources: Fine-tuning large LLMs can be computationally expensive. Consider using cloud-based resources or specialized hardware.

Overfitting: Be mindful of overfitting, where the LLM becomes too specialized to the training data and performs poorly on unseen data.

By fine-tuning LLMs, you can create RAG systems that are highly effective for specific tasks and domains, leading to more accurate, relevant, and efficient information retrieval and generation.

Chapter 6

Developing a RAG-Powered Question Answering System

You're diving into a critical part of building a successful RAG-powered question answering system! Before we can even retrieve relevant information, we need to understand what the user is asking. Here's a breakdown of query understanding and processing:

6.1 Query Understanding and Processing

The first step in any question answering system is to understand the user's query. This involves taking the user's natural language question and transforming it into a format that can be used for retrieval and answer generation.

1. Natural Language Understanding (NLU)

Intent Recognition: Determine the user's intent. What are they trying to achieve with their question? Are they seeking a factual answer, a definition, a comparison, or an opinion?

Entity Extraction: Identify key entities (people, places, things, concepts) mentioned in the query. This helps to focus the search and retrieval process.

Relationship Extraction: Understand the relationships between entities in the query. For example, in the query "Who is the CEO of Google?", the relationship is "CEO of" between the entities "Who" (which implies a person) and "Google."

2. Query Processing Techniques

Tokenization: Break down the query into individual words or sub-words (tokens).

Stop Word Removal: Remove common words (like "the," "a," "is") that don't carry much meaning.

Stemming and Lemmatization: Reduce words to their root form (e.g., "running" to "run") to improve matching and retrieval.

Part-of-Speech Tagging: Identify the grammatical role of each word (noun, verb, adjective, etc.) to understand the structure of the query.

Named Entity Recognition (NER): Identify and classify named entities (like people, organizations, locations) in the query.

3. Query Expansion

Synonyms and Related Terms: Expand the query with synonyms or related terms to broaden the search and improve recall.

Query Rewriting: Rephrase the query to improve its clarity or to better match the language used in the knowledge base.

4. Example: Processing a Query

Let's say the user asks: "What are the health benefits of eating apples?"

Tokenization: ["What," "are," "the," "health," "benefits," "of," "eating," "apples?"]

Stop Word Removal: ["health," "benefits," "eating," "apples"]

Lemmatization: ["health," "benefit," "eat," "apple"]

Entity Extraction: "health benefits," "apple"

Relationship Extraction: The relationship is between "health benefits" and "apple" (i.e., the benefits of eating apples).

5. Tools and Libraries

NLTK: The Natural Language Toolkit provides tools for tokenization, stemming, lemmatization, and part-of-speech tagging.

spaCy: A powerful library for natural language processing, offering features like named entity recognition and dependency parsing.

Hugging Face Transformers: Provides access to pre-trained models for various NLU tasks.

By carefully processing and understanding the user's query, you can lay the groundwork for accurate and relevant information retrieval in your RAG-powered question answering system.

6.2 Retrieval and Ranking of Relevant Information

Once you've understood the user's query, the next step is to retrieve the most relevant information from your knowledge base. This involves searching, filtering, and ranking candidate documents or chunks of information.

1. Retrieval Techniques

Dense Retrieval:

Semantic Similarity: Use embedding models to represent the query and documents as vectors and find documents with high cosine similarity to the query embedding.

Vector Databases: Utilize vector databases like FAISS, Milvus, or Pinecone for efficient similarity search.

Sparse Retrieval:

Keyword Matching: Identify documents that share keywords with the query, potentially using TF-IDF scores to weigh the importance of keywords.

BM25: A more advanced ranking function that considers term frequency, document length, and other factors.

Hybrid Retrieval:

Combine Dense and Sparse: Leverage the strengths of both approaches by combining their scores or using a two-stage retrieval process.

2. Ranking Strategies

Relevance Score: Use a combination of factors to calculate a relevance score for each document, such as:

Similarity Score: Cosine similarity for dense retrieval, TF-IDF or BM25 scores for sparse retrieval.

Metadata: Consider document metadata like recency, popularity, or source authority.

Query-Document Matching: Analyze the extent of overlap between the query and the document, including the presence of key entities or relationships.

Ranking Algorithms:

Simple Ranking: Sort documents by their relevance score in descending order.

Learning to Rank: Train machine learning models to rank documents based on features extracted from the query and documents.

3. Filtering and Refinement

Keyword Filtering: Filter out documents that don't contain essential keywords from the query.

Semantic Filtering: Use dense retrieval to filter out documents that are not semantically related to the query.

Diversity: Promote diversity in the results by including documents from different sources or perspectives.

4. Example: Retrieval and Ranking with Haystack

Haystack provides a framework for building question answering pipelines that include retrieval and ranking components.

Python

```python
from haystack.document_stores import InMemoryDocumentStore

from haystack.nodes import EmbeddingRetriever, FARMReader


# Initialize the document store and retriever

document_store = InMemoryDocumentStore()

retriever = EmbeddingRetriever(document_store=document_store)


# ... (Code to load and index documents) ...


# Retrieve relevant documents

retrieved_docs = retriever.retrieve(query="What is the capital of France?")


# ... (Code to use a reader to extract the answer from the retrieved documents) ...
```

5. Optimizing Retrieval and Ranking

Experiment with Different Techniques: Try different retrieval and ranking methods to see what works best for your data and application.

Evaluate Performance: Use metrics like precision, recall, and mean average precision (MAP) to evaluate the effectiveness of your retrieval and ranking system.

Fine-tune Parameters: Adjust parameters like the number of documents to retrieve, similarity thresholds, or weighting factors to optimize performance.

By implementing effective retrieval and ranking strategies, you can ensure that your RAG-powered question answering system finds and prioritizes the most relevant information to generate accurate and informative answers.

6.3 Generating Accurate and Informative Answers

This stage involves taking the retrieved information and the user's query, and then using an LLM to generate a well-formed, comprehensive, and accurate answer. Here's a breakdown of the key considerations:

1. Answer Extraction vs. Generation

Extraction: If the answer is explicitly stated in the retrieved documents, you might be able to extract it directly. This is often done using techniques like named entity recognition, relation extraction, or question-answering models that identify answer spans within text.

Generation: In many cases, the answer needs to be synthesized from multiple pieces of information or presented in a way that's tailored to the user's query. This is where the LLM's generative capabilities shine.

2. Crafting Effective Prompts

Provide Context: Include the most relevant retrieved information in the prompt to ground the LLM's response.

Clearly State the Question: Ensure the prompt clearly presents the question that needs to be answered.

Guide the Output: Provide instructions on the desired format, length, and style of the answer.

3. LLM Techniques for Answer Generation

Fine-tuned LLMs: Use LLMs that have been fine-tuned for question answering or the specific domain of your knowledge base.

Few-Shot Learning: Provide a few examples of question-answer pairs in the prompt to guide the LLM.

Chain-of-Thought Prompting: Encourage the LLM to generate a step-by-step reasoning process before providing the answer.

4. Ensuring Answer Quality

Accuracy: Verify that the generated answer is factually correct and consistent with the retrieved information.

Completeness: Ensure the answer addresses all aspects of the user's query.

Clarity and Conciseness: Present the answer in a clear, concise, and easy-to-understand manner.

Relevance: Ensure the answer is directly relevant to the user's question and avoids extraneous information.

5. Example: Answer Generation with LangChain

LangChain's `RetrievalQA` chain simplifies the process of retrieving information and generating answers:

Python

```python
from langchain.chains import RetrievalQA

from langchain.llms import OpenAI



# ... (Code to set up the retriever and LLM) ...



qa_chain = RetrievalQA.from_chain_type(llm=OpenAI(), retriever=retriever)



query = "What is the capital of France?"

result = qa_chain({"query": query})

print(result['result'])  # Output: Paris
```

6. Handling Uncertainty

Confidence Scores: If possible, provide a confidence score with the answer to indicate the LLM's certainty.

Fallback Mechanisms: If the LLM is unable to generate a confident answer, provide a fallback mechanism, such as returning the most relevant retrieved documents or prompting the user to rephrase their query.

By carefully combining retrieval, prompt engineering, and LLM generation techniques, you can create a RAG-powered question answering system that provides accurate, informative, and satisfying answers to your users.

Chapter 7

Building a RAG-Based Chatbot

7.1 Designing Conversational Flows

A successful chatbot needs more than just the ability to answer questions. It needs to engage users in natural, flowing conversations that feel intuitive and helpful. This is where designing conversational flows comes in.

1. Understanding Conversational Flow

A Guided Journey: A conversational flow is a structured path that guides the user through a conversation with the chatbot. It anticipates user inputs and provides appropriate responses, creating a dynamic and interactive experience.

Key Elements:

Intents: The user's intentions or goals in the conversation.

Entities: Key pieces of information relevant to the conversation (e.g., names, dates, locations, product names).

Dialog Turns: The back-and-forth exchanges between the user and the chatbot.

Context: The ongoing information and history of the conversation.

Visualizing the Flow: Conversational flows are often visualized using diagrams or flowcharts to map out the different paths and branches in the conversation.

2. Designing Effective Flows

Start with a Clear Goal: Define the primary purpose of your chatbot. What problems should it solve? What tasks should it help users accomplish?

Identify User Personas: Understand your target audience. What are their needs, expectations, and communication styles?

Create a Chatbot Persona: Give your chatbot a personality that aligns with your brand and resonates with your users.

Map Out the Conversation: Outline the main paths and branches of the conversation. Anticipate user questions and provide appropriate responses.

Handle Unexpected Input: Design strategies for handling unexpected user input or questions that fall outside the defined flow.

Keep it Concise and Engaging: Use clear, concise language and avoid long blocks of text. Incorporate elements like emojis, GIFs, or buttons to make the conversation more engaging.

3. Tools for Designing Conversational Flows

Flowcharting Tools: Draw.io, Lucidchart, or Miro can be used to create visual representations of your conversational flows.

Chatbot Design Platforms: Many platforms like Dialogflow, Rasa, or Botpress provide tools for designing and managing conversational flows.

LangChain: You can use LangChain to manage the flow of conversation and integrate with LLMs for generating dynamic responses.

4. Example: A Simple Conversational Flow

Imagine a chatbot for ordering pizza:

User: "I want to order a pizza."

Chatbot: "Great! What kind of pizza would you like?"

User: "Pepperoni."

Chatbot: "What size?"

User: "Large."

Chatbot: "Okay, a large pepperoni pizza. Anything else?"

User: "No, that's all."

Chatbot: "Great! Your order will be ready in 30 minutes."

5. Iterate and Improve

Test and Gather Feedback: Test your conversational flows with real users and gather feedback to identify areas for improvement.

Analyze Chat Logs: Analyze chat logs to understand user behavior and identify common questions or issues.

Continuously Refine: Continuously refine your conversational flows based on user feedback and data analysis to create a more engaging and effective chatbot experience.

By carefully designing your conversational flows, you can create RAG-powered chatbots that are not only informative but also engaging, helpful, and enjoyable to interact with.

7.2 Contextual Memory and Multi-turn Dialogues

Imagine having a conversation with someone who forgets everything you said just a moment ago. It would be frustrating and unproductive, right? The same applies to chatbots. Contextual memory is the ability of a chatbot to remember and utilize information from previous turns in the conversation, making the interaction feel more natural, coherent, and personalized.

1. Why Contextual Memory Matters

Coherent Conversations: Remembering past interactions helps the chatbot maintain coherence and avoid repetitive or irrelevant responses.

Personalized Experience: By recalling user preferences or past requests, the chatbot can provide more personalized and relevant answers.

Complex Tasks: Contextual memory enables the chatbot to handle complex tasks that require multiple steps or information gathering over several turns.

2. Implementing Contextual Memory

Conversation History: Store the history of the conversation, including user inputs and chatbot responses.

State Management: Maintain a "state" for each user, representing the current context of the conversation (e.g., the topic being discussed, the user's goal, or any relevant information gathered).

Memory Mechanisms:

Simple Memory: Store the conversation history as a list or a string.

Key-Value Memory: Store specific pieces of information as key-value pairs (e.g., "user_name": "John").

Vector Database Memory: Store embeddings of past interactions to capture semantic context.

3. Multi-turn Dialogue Management

Dialogue State Tracking: Keep track of the current state of the dialogue, including the user's goals, the information exchanged, and any pending actions.

Turn-Taking: Manage the flow of the conversation, ensuring smooth transitions between user turns and chatbot responses.

Contextual Response Generation: Use the context from previous turns to generate more relevant and informative responses.

4. Example: Using Contextual Memory in LangChain

LangChain provides a `ConversationChain` that allows you to maintain conversation history and use it to generate responses:

Python

```python
from langchain.chains import ConversationChain

from langchain.llms import OpenAI


llm = OpenAI(temperature=0)

conversation = ConversationChain(llm=llm)


# Start the conversation

response    =    conversation.predict(input="Hi there!")

print(response)


# Continue the conversation

response = conversation.predict(input="What's the weather like in Paris?")

print(response)   # The LLM will have access to the previous turn
```

5. Challenges and Considerations

Memory Limitations: Balancing the amount of context to store with memory constraints and processing efficiency.

Ambiguity and Coreference Resolution: Handling ambiguous language and correctly resolving references to entities mentioned in previous turns.

Privacy: Protecting user data and ensuring compliance with privacy regulations.

By effectively implementing contextual memory and multi-turn dialogue management, you can create RAG-powered chatbots that engage in natural, coherent, and personalized conversations, leading to a more satisfying and helpful user experience.

7.3 Integrating with Messaging Platforms

Building a great chatbot is just the first step. To truly reach your audience, you need to integrate it with popular messaging platforms like WhatsApp, Facebook Messenger, Slack, or Telegram. This allows users to interact with your chatbot seamlessly within their preferred communication channels.

1. Choosing the Right Platform

Target Audience: Where do your target users spend most of their time? Which platforms are most popular in your industry or region?

Platform Features: Consider the features offered by each platform. Some platforms offer more advanced functionalities like rich media support, interactive buttons, or payment integration.

Development Resources: Evaluate the development tools and APIs provided by each platform. Some platforms have more mature and well-documented APIs.

2. Integration Methods

Platform-Specific APIs: Most messaging platforms offer APIs that allow you to send and receive messages programmatically. You'll need to use the platform's SDK or libraries to interact with these APIs.

Chatbot Building Platforms: Platforms like Dialogflow, Rasa, or Botpress often provide built-in integrations with popular messaging platforms, simplifying the process.

LangChain Integrations: LangChain is starting to offer integrations with messaging platforms, allowing you to connect your chatbot logic with the platform's API.

3. Integration Steps

1 Create a Chatbot Account: Set up a developer account on the messaging platform and create a new chatbot application.

2 Obtain API Credentials: Get the necessary API credentials (like API keys or tokens) to authenticate your chatbot with the platform.

3 Implement API Calls: Use the platform's API to send and receive messages. This typically involves making HTTP requests to the platform's servers.

4 Handle Webhooks: Configure webhooks to receive incoming messages from the platform. Webhooks are notifications sent by the platform to your server when a user interacts with your chatbot.

5 Connect to Your Chatbot Logic: Connect the platform's API to your chatbot's logic, which may involve using a chatbot building platform or custom code with LangChain.

4. Example: Integrating with WhatsApp

To integrate with WhatsApp, you would use the WhatsApp Business API:

1 Sign up for WhatsApp Business API: Apply for access to the API through a WhatsApp Business Solution Provider.

2 Get API Credentials: Obtain your API credentials, including your phone number ID and access token.

4 Use the Twilio API for WhatsApp: Twilio is a popular provider that offers a convenient way to interact with the WhatsApp Business API. You can use their Python library to send and receive messages.

5 Set up Webhooks: Configure a webhook URL to receive incoming messages from WhatsApp.

6 Connect to Your Chatbot: Process incoming messages, generate responses using your RAG system, and send replies back through the Twilio API.

5. Considerations

Platform-Specific Requirements: Each platform has its own set of requirements and guidelines for chatbot development. Be sure to familiarize yourself with these guidelines.

User Experience: Design your chatbot interactions to provide a seamless and intuitive user experience within the messaging platform.

Scalability: Ensure your integration can handle a large volume of messages and users as your chatbot grows in popularity.

By integrating your RAG-powered chatbot with messaging platforms, you can make it easily accessible to a wider audience, increasing its reach and impact.

Chapter 8

Generating Text with RAG

8.1 Summarization and Paraphrasing

RAG empowers you to go beyond simple retrieval and question answering. You can use it to generate new text that summarizes or paraphrases information from your knowledge base, making complex information more accessible and digestible.

1. Summarization

Condensing Information: Summarization involves creating a shorter version of a text that captures its main points while omitting less important details.

Types of Summarization:

Extractive Summarization: Selecting the most important sentences or phrases from the original text to form the summary.

Abstractive Summarization: Generating new sentences that capture the essence of the original text in a more concise and potentially rephrased manner.

Applications:

Document Summarization: Creating summaries of long articles, reports, or documents.

Meeting Summarization: Generating concise summaries of meeting transcripts.

News Summarization: Providing short summaries of news articles.

2. Paraphrasing

Rephrasing Text: Paraphrasing involves expressing the same information in a different way, often using alternative words or sentence structures.

Maintaining Meaning: The goal is to preserve the original meaning while making the text more accessible, clearer, or more suitable for a specific audience.

Applications:

Simplifying Complex Text: Making technical or academic writing easier to understand.

Avoiding Plagiarism: Restating information from sources in your own words.

Adapting Text to Different Contexts: Tailoring the language and style of a text for a specific audience or purpose.

3. RAG for Summarization and Paraphrasing

Retrieval: Retrieve relevant documents or sections of text from your knowledge base.

Prompt Engineering: Craft prompts that clearly instruct the LLM to summarize or paraphrase the retrieved information.

LLM Generation: Utilize the LLM's ability to understand and generate natural language to create the summary or paraphrase.

4. Example: Summarization with LangChain

Python

```
from          langchain.chains.summarize          import
load_summarize_chain

from langchain.llms import OpenAI
```

```
# ... (Code to set up the retriever and LLM) ...


# Load the summarization chain

chain                                                =
load_summarize_chain(OpenAI(temperature=0),
chain_type="map_reduce")


# Retrieve a document from your knowledge base

docs = retriever.get_relevant_documents("What is
the history of the Eiffel Tower?")


# Generate the summary

summary = chain.run(docs)

print(summary)
```

5. Tips for Effective Summarization and Paraphrasing

Focus on the Main Points: Identify the most important information in the text.

Use Concise Language: Avoid unnecessary words or phrases.

Maintain Clarity: Ensure the summary or paraphrase is easy to understand.

Preserve the Original Meaning: Avoid introducing new information or changing the meaning of the original text.

By combining RAG with powerful LLMs, you can create tools that effectively summarize and paraphrase information, making complex knowledge more accessible and useful for various applications.

8.2 Creative Writing and Content Generation

RAG can be a powerful tool for creative writing and content generation, helping you overcome writer's block, explore new ideas, and produce engaging content in various formats.

1. Breaking Writer's Block

Idea Generation: Use RAG to brainstorm ideas by retrieving relevant information, exploring different perspectives, or generating prompts for creative writing.

Overcoming Stalls: When you're stuck in your writing, RAG can help you find new directions, generate alternative storylines, or develop your characters.

2. Generating Different Creative Text Formats

Stories: Create short stories, novels, or scripts by providing RAG with prompts, characters, and plot points.

Poems: Generate poems in different styles by providing RAG with themes, keywords, or rhyming patterns.

Scripts: Write scripts for plays, movies, or video games by using RAG to develop dialogues, scenes, and characters.

Song Lyrics: Compose song lyrics by providing RAG with melodies, themes, or emotions.

3. Content Creation for Various Purposes

Blog Posts: Generate blog posts on various topics by providing RAG with outlines, keywords, or research articles.

Articles: Write articles for websites, magazines, or newspapers by using RAG to gather information and structure the content.

Marketing Copy: Create compelling marketing copy for advertisements, social media posts, or websites by providing RAG with product descriptions and target audience information.

4. Using RAG for Creative Inspiration

Explore Different Styles: Provide RAG with examples of different writing styles to inspire your own writing.

Combine Ideas: Use RAG to combine seemingly unrelated concepts or ideas to spark creativity.

Build on Existing Works: Provide RAG with existing stories, poems, or scripts to generate new variations or sequels.

5. Example: Generating a Story Idea with RAG

Provide RAG with a prompt like: "A young detective investigates a mysterious disappearance in a futuristic city." RAG can then retrieve information about detective stories, futuristic settings, and missing person cases, and use this information to generate a unique story idea, including characters, plot points, and potential twists.

6. Ethical Considerations

Originality and Plagiarism: Ensure that the generated content is original and doesn't plagiarize existing works.

Bias and Discrimination: Be mindful of potential biases in the training data of the LLM and ensure that the generated content is fair and inclusive.

Transparency: Be transparent about the use of RAG in the content generation process.

By using RAG creatively and responsibly, you can unlock new possibilities for creative writing and content generation, producing engaging and original content in various formats.

8.3 Creative Writing and Content Generation

RAG can be a powerful tool for creative writing and content generation, helping you overcome writer's block, explore new ideas, and produce engaging content in various formats.

1. Breaking Writer's Block

Idea Generation: Use RAG to brainstorm ideas by retrieving relevant information, exploring different perspectives, or generating prompts for creative writing.

Overcoming Stalls: When you're stuck in your writing, RAG can help you find new directions, generate alternative storylines, or develop your characters.

2. Generating Different Creative Text Formats

Stories: Create short stories, novels, or scripts by providing RAG with prompts, characters, and plot points.

Poems: Generate poems in different styles by providing RAG with themes, keywords, or rhyming patterns.

Scripts: Write scripts for plays, movies, or video games by using RAG to develop dialogues, scenes, and characters.

Song Lyrics: Compose song lyrics by providing RAG with melodies, themes, or emotions.

3. Content Creation for Various Purposes

Blog Posts: Generate blog posts on various topics by providing RAG with outlines, keywords, or research articles.

Articles: Write articles for websites, magazines, or newspapers by using RAG to gather information and structure the content.

Marketing Copy: Create compelling marketing copy for advertisements, social media posts, or websites by providing RAG with product descriptions and target audience information.

4. Using RAG for Creative Inspiration

Explore Different Styles: Provide RAG with examples of different writing styles to inspire your own writing.

Combine Ideas: Use RAG to combine seemingly unrelated concepts or ideas to spark creativity.

Build on Existing Works: Provide RAG with existing stories, poems, or scripts to generate new variations or sequels.

5. Example: Generating a Story Idea with RAG

Provide RAG with a prompt like: "A young detective investigates a mysterious disappearance in a futuristic city." RAG can then retrieve information about detective stories, futuristic settings, and missing person cases, and use this information to generate a unique story idea, including characters, plot points, and potential twists.

6. Ethical Considerations

Originality and Plagiarism: Ensure that the generated content is original and doesn't plagiarize existing works.

Bias and Discrimination: Be mindful of potential biases in the training data of the LLM and ensure that the generated content is fair and inclusive.

Transparency: Be transparent about the use of RAG in the content generation process.

By using RAG creatively and responsibly, you can unlock new possibilities for creative writing and content generation, producing engaging and original content in various formats.

Chapter 9

Advanced RAG Techniques

9.1 Multi-hop Reasoning and Knowledge Graph Integration

1. Multi-hop Reasoning

Beyond Single Connections: Traditional question answering often focuses on finding answers that are directly linked to the keywords in the question. Multi-hop reasoning goes beyond this by considering multiple steps or "hops" through the knowledge base to find the answer.

Example: Consider the question "Who is the CEO of the company that manufactures the iPhone?" Answering this requires multiple hops:

Identify "iPhone" as a product.

Find the manufacturer of the iPhone (Apple).

Identify the CEO of Apple (Tim Cook).

Challenges:

Identifying Relevant Hops: Determining which connections or relationships in the knowledge base are relevant to the question.

Combining Information: Integrating information from multiple hops to arrive at the final answer.

2. Knowledge Graph Integration

Structured Knowledge: A knowledge graph is a structured representation of knowledge that consists of entities (nodes) and the relationships (edges) between them. This structure makes it ideal for multi-hop reasoning.

Example: In a knowledge graph, "iPhone" might be an entity with a "manufactured_by" relationship to the entity "Apple," which in turn has a "ceo" relationship to the entity "Tim Cook."

Benefits:

Efficient Reasoning: Knowledge graphs provide a clear and organized way to traverse relationships between entities.

Complex Question Answering: Enables answering questions that require understanding complex relationships and dependencies.

Explainability: The reasoning process can be traced through the knowledge graph, making the answers more transparent and interpretable.

3. Combining RAG with Knowledge Graphs

Retrieval: Use the question to identify relevant entities and relationships in the knowledge graph.

Graph Traversal: Traverse the knowledge graph to find paths that connect the entities and answer the question.

LLM Integration: Use the LLM to generate natural language answers based on the information extracted from the knowledge graph.

4. Example: Using a Knowledge Graph for Question Answering

Imagine a knowledge graph with information about movies, actors, and directors. You could use this knowledge graph to answer questions like:

"Who directed the movie Inception?"

"Which movies have both Leonardo DiCaprio and Tom Hanks starred in?"

"Who are the actors that have worked with Steven Spielberg?"

5. Tools and Libraries

Neo4j: A popular graph database for storing and querying knowledge graphs.

NetworkX: A Python library for creating, manipulating, and analyzing graphs.

RDFlib: A Python library for working with RDF (Resource Description Framework) data, a common format for knowledge graphs.

6. Challenges and Considerations

Knowledge Graph Construction: Building and maintaining a comprehensive and accurate knowledge graph can be challenging.

Scalability: Handling large and complex knowledge graphs efficiently.

Integration with LLMs: Seamlessly integrating knowledge graph traversal with LLM-based answer generation.

By integrating RAG with knowledge graphs and multi-hop reasoning, you can create powerful question answering systems that can handle complex questions and provide more insightful and explainable answers.

9.2 Handling Uncertainty and Ambiguity

RAG systems need to be able to gracefully handle situations where the information they retrieve is uncertain or ambiguous. This involves recognizing limitations, quantifying confidence, and providing useful responses even when faced with incomplete or conflicting information.

1. Sources of Uncertainty and Ambiguity

Ambiguous Queries: User questions can be vague, open-ended, or have multiple possible interpretations.

Incomplete Knowledge: The knowledge base may not contain all the necessary information to answer the question definitively.

Conflicting Information: Different sources in the knowledge base may provide contradictory information.

Noisy Data: The data may contain errors, inconsistencies, or outdated information.

2. Techniques for Handling Uncertainty

Confidence Estimation:

LLM Confidence Scores: Many LLMs provide confidence scores or probabilities associated with their generated outputs. Use these scores to assess the certainty of the answer.

Ensemble Methods: Combine the outputs of multiple LLMs or retrieval methods to get a more robust estimate of confidence.

Uncertainty-Aware Prompting:

Explicitly Acknowledge Uncertainty: Incorporate phrases like "Based on the available information..." or "It's possible that..." in the prompt to acknowledge uncertainty.

Request Justification: Ask the LLM to provide justification or evidence for its answer, which can help assess its confidence.

Handling Contradictions:

Identify and Highlight Discrepancies: If contradictory information is retrieved, explicitly highlight the discrepancies to the user.

Present Multiple Perspectives: Offer multiple possible answers or interpretations, reflecting the different perspectives found in the knowledge base.

Fallback Mechanisms:

Return Relevant Sources: If a confident answer cannot be generated, provide the user with the most relevant retrieved sources, allowing them to assess the information themselves.

Ask for Clarification: Prompt the user to rephrase their query or provide more information if the initial question is ambiguous.

3. Example: Handling Uncertainty in a Medical Diagnosis Chatbot

Imagine a chatbot that helps users with potential medical diagnoses. If a user describes symptoms that could indicate multiple conditions, the chatbot should:

Acknowledge Uncertainty: "Based on your symptoms, it's possible that you have..."

Provide a Range of Possibilities: "...a common cold, the flu, or allergies."

Recommend Further Action: "It's important to consult a doctor for a proper diagnosis."

4. Benefits of Handling Uncertainty

Increased Trust: Acknowledging uncertainty builds trust with users by demonstrating that the system is aware of its limitations.

Improved User Experience: Providing context and alternative perspectives helps users make informed decisions.

Reduced Risk: Avoiding definitive answers in uncertain situations can help reduce the risk of providing incorrect or harmful information.

By incorporating techniques for handling uncertainty and ambiguity, you can create more robust and reliable RAG systems that provide useful responses even when faced with incomplete or conflicting information.

9.3 Explainability and Interpretability

Explainability and interpretability are closely related concepts that focus on making AI systems more transparent and understandable to humans. This is particularly important in RAG, where the combination of retrieval and generation can make it difficult to trace how the system arrived at a particular answer.

1. Explainability

Providing the "Why": Explainability focuses on providing insights into *why* an AI system made a specific decision or generated a particular output. It's about understanding the reasoning behind the system's behavior.

Techniques for Explainability in RAG:

Highlighting Source Documents: Indicate which documents from the knowledge base were used to generate the answer.

Showing Relevant Snippets: Display the specific text passages that support the answer.

Explaining Retrieval and Ranking: Provide information about how the relevant documents were retrieved and ranked.

Visualizing the Reasoning Process: Use diagrams or flowcharts to illustrate the steps involved in generating the answer.

2. Interpretability

Understanding the "How": Interpretability focuses on understanding *how* an AI system works internally. It's about gaining insights into the model's decision-making process and the factors that influence its output.

Challenges in LLMs: Large language models are often considered "black boxes" due to their complex internal workings. It can be difficult to understand how they process information and generate text.

Techniques for Interpretability in RAG:

Attention Mechanisms: Analyze the attention weights of the LLM to understand which parts of the input text it focused on.

Probing: Use probes or probes to analyze the internal representations of the LLM and understand how it encodes information.

Simplified Models: Use simpler, more interpretable models for certain parts of the RAG system, such as for retrieval or ranking.

3. Why Explainability and Interpretability Matter

Building Trust: Transparent AI systems are more likely to be trusted by users.

Debugging and Improvement: Understanding how the system works helps identify errors, biases, or areas for improvement.

Accountability: Explainable AI systems are more accountable because their decisions can be traced and understood.

Ethical Considerations: Ensuring fairness, avoiding bias, and preventing unintended consequences requires understanding how the AI system works.

4. Example: Explainable Question Answering

Imagine a RAG system that answers questions about historical events. An explainable system might provide an answer like this:

"The French Revolution began in 1789. (Source: *A History of the French Revolution* by Thomas Carlyle).

This book states that the storming of the Bastille on July 14, 1789, marked the beginning of the revolution."

This explanation shows the source of the information and the specific text passage that supports the answer.

5. Tools and Libraries

LangChain: Provides tools for tracking and displaying the source documents used in RAG.

Captum: A library for interpreting PyTorch models, including techniques for analyzing attention mechanisms.

Alibi: A library for explaining machine learning models, including methods for generating counterfactual explanations.

By incorporating explainability and interpretability into your RAG systems, you can create more transparent, trustworthy, and accountable AI applications.

Chapter 10

Deploying and Scaling Your RAG

10.1 Optimizing for Performance and Efficiency

Performance and efficiency are critical for any application, but especially for RAG systems that often deal with large amounts of data and complex processing. Optimizing your RAG system ensures a smooth user experience, reduces costs, and allows your application to scale effectively.

1. Retrieval Optimization

Efficient Indexing:

Vector Databases: Utilize vector databases like FAISS, Milvus, or Pinecone that are optimized for fast similarity search.

Indexing Techniques: Choose appropriate indexing techniques (e.g., HNSW, IVF) based on your data size and performance requirements.

Caching:

Store Frequently Accessed Data: Cache frequently accessed embeddings or documents in memory to reduce retrieval time.

Filtering:

Pre-filtering: Use techniques like keyword filtering or BM25 to quickly narrow down the search space before performing more computationally expensive dense retrieval.

Batching:

Combine Queries: Batch multiple queries together to reduce the overhead of individual requests to the vector database.

2. Language Model Optimization

Model Selection:

Right-Sized Models: Choose LLMs that are appropriately sized for your task and computational resources. Smaller models can be faster and more efficient.

Distilled Models: Consider using distilled versions of larger models, which offer comparable performance with reduced size and latency.

Prompt Optimization:

Concise Prompts: Keep prompts clear and concise to reduce the amount of text the LLM needs to process.

Prompt Templates: Use prompt templates to avoid redundant computations and improve consistency.

Caching:

Cache LLM Responses: Cache responses for common queries or prompts to avoid redundant computations.

3. Code Optimization

Efficient Data Structures: Use efficient data structures like dictionaries or sets for storing and accessing data.

Asynchronous Programming: Utilize asynchronous programming techniques to perform multiple tasks concurrently, such as retrieval and generation.

Profiling and Monitoring:

Identify Bottlenecks: Use profiling tools to identify performance bottlenecks in your code.

Monitor Performance: Continuously monitor the performance of your RAG system to identify areas for improvement.

4. Infrastructure Optimization

Hardware:

GPUs: Utilize GPUs to accelerate computationally intensive tasks like embedding generation and similarity search.

Optimized Servers: Choose servers with sufficient memory and processing power to handle your workload.

Cloud Services:

Managed Services: Consider using managed services for vector databases, LLMs, or other components to reduce infrastructure management overhead.

Scaling:

Horizontal Scaling: Scale your application horizontally by adding more servers to handle increased traffic.

5. Tools and Libraries

LangChain: Provides tools for optimizing retrieval and LLM interaction.

Haystack: Offers features for optimizing question answering pipelines.

FAISS: Includes optimized algorithms and GPU support for efficient similarity search.

Profiling Tools: Use Python's built-in `cProfile` module or other profiling tools to analyze code performance.

By implementing these optimization strategies, you can ensure that your RAG system performs efficiently, provides a smooth user experience, and scales effectively to handle growing demands.

10.2 Cloud Deployment Strategies

Deploying your RAG application to the cloud offers numerous benefits, including scalability, reliability, and cost-effectiveness. Here are some key strategies to consider:

1. Platform as a Service (PaaS)

Focus on Application Logic: PaaS providers (like Google App Engine, AWS Elastic Beanstalk, or Heroku) manage the underlying infrastructure, allowing you to focus on deploying your application code.

Benefits:

Ease of Deployment: Simplified deployment process, often with built-in tools and automation.

Scalability: Easy to scale resources up or down based on demand.

Cost-Effectiveness: Pay-as-you-go pricing models can be cost-effective, especially for variable workloads.

Considerations:

Vendor Lock-in: May lead to vendor lock-in with a specific cloud provider.

Limited Control: Less control over the underlying infrastructure compared to IaaS.

2. Infrastructure as a Service (IaaS)

Full Infrastructure Control: IaaS providers (like AWS EC2, Google Compute Engine, or Azure Virtual Machines) give you more control over the underlying infrastructure, allowing you to customize the environment to your specific needs.

Benefits:

Flexibility: Greater flexibility in choosing operating systems, configurations, and software.

Customization: Ability to tailor the infrastructure to specific performance or security requirements.

Considerations:

Increased Management Overhead: Requires more infrastructure management compared to PaaS.

Higher Costs: Can be more expensive, especially for complex setups or if not managed efficiently.

3. Containerization

Packaging for Portability: Containerization (using Docker) packages your application and its dependencies into a portable container that can be easily deployed across different environments.

Benefits:

Consistency: Ensures consistency across development, testing, and production environments.

Portability: Easily move the application between different cloud providers or on-premises servers.

Efficiency: Containers are lightweight and can be easily scaled.

Orchestration:

Kubernetes: Use Kubernetes to manage and orchestrate containerized deployments, enabling automated scaling, rolling updates, and self-healing.

4. Serverless Computing

Focus on Functions: Serverless platforms (like AWS Lambda, Google Cloud Functions, or Azure Functions) allow you to deploy individual functions or microservices that are triggered by events.

Benefits:

Scalability and Cost-Efficiency: Automatically scales based on demand, and you only pay for the resources used.

Reduced Operational Overhead: No need to manage servers or infrastructure.

Considerations:

Cold Starts: May experience latency due to cold starts when a function is invoked for the first time.

Vendor Lock-in: Can lead to vendor lock-in with a specific serverless platform.

5. Deployment Tools and Strategies

Continuous Integration/Continuous Deployment (CI/CD): Automate the build, testing, and deployment process to ensure rapid and reliable deployments.

Infrastructure as Code (IaC): Use tools like Terraform or CloudFormation to define and manage your infrastructure in a declarative manner.

Monitoring and Logging: Implement monitoring and logging tools to track the performance and health of your deployed application.

By carefully considering these cloud deployment strategies and utilizing the right tools, you can make your RAG application accessible, scalable, and reliable for your users.

10.3 Monitoring and Maintenance

Deploying your RAG application is just the beginning. Continuous monitoring and regular maintenance are crucial to ensure its ongoing performance, reliability, and accuracy.

1. Monitoring

Performance Metrics:

Latency: Track the time it takes to respond to user queries.

Accuracy: Measure the accuracy of answers generated by the system.

Retrieval Effectiveness: Monitor the recall and precision of the retrieval process.

Error Rates: Track the frequency of errors or unexpected behavior.

System Health:

Resource Utilization: Monitor CPU usage, memory consumption, and storage space.

API Usage: Track API calls and usage limits for external services (e.g., LLMs, vector databases).

Uptime and Availability: Ensure the application is available and responsive to users.

User Feedback:

Collect User Feedback: Gather feedback from users on the quality and helpfulness of the responses.

Analyze Chat Logs: Review conversation logs to identify common issues or areas for improvement.

Monitoring Tools:

Cloud Monitoring Services: Utilize cloud provider monitoring tools (e.g., Google Cloud Monitoring, AWS CloudWatch, Azure Monitor) to track metrics and set alerts.

Logging Frameworks: Use logging frameworks to record events and errors for analysis.

Visualization Tools: Visualize performance data using dashboards or graphs to identify trends and anomalies.

2. Maintenance

Data Updates:

Regularly Update Knowledge Base: Keep your knowledge base up-to-date with the latest information.

Re-index Data: Re-index the data after updates to ensure efficient retrieval.

Model Updates:

Fine-tune LLMs: Periodically fine-tune your LLMs with new data or feedback to improve their performance.

Upgrade to New Models: Consider upgrading to newer, more powerful LLMs as they become available.

Software Updates:

Update Dependencies: Regularly update libraries and dependencies to benefit from bug fixes and performance improvements.

Security Patches: Apply security patches promptly to protect against vulnerabilities.

Code Refactoring:

Improve Code Quality: Refactor code to improve readability, maintainability, and efficiency.

Backup and Recovery:

Regular Backups: Perform regular backups of your data and application to prevent data loss.

Disaster Recovery Plan: Have a disaster recovery plan in place to ensure business continuity in case of unexpected events.

3. Automation

Automate Monitoring: Set up automated alerts for critical metrics or events.

Automate Updates: Automate data updates, model retraining, and software deployments whenever possible.

Automated Testing: Implement automated tests to ensure the quality and reliability of your application after updates or changes.

By implementing a comprehensive monitoring and maintenance plan, you can ensure that your RAG system remains accurate, efficient, and reliable over time, providing a consistently positive experience for your users.